The Campus History Series

ST. MARY'S HALL
AND DOANE ACADEMY

For at least 75 years after the opening of the boarding school known as St. Mary's Hall, the horse and carriage was one of the three main modes of transportation to and from the school, the others being steam locomotive and steamboat or sailboat. Yet hundreds of parents from across the continent and beyond sent their daughters over the oceans, mountains, plains, rivers, and dirt roads to become a part of Bishop Doane's "great experiment." This is the story of that school. (Courtesy Eliza G. Doane Archival Library, Doane Academy.)

ON THE FRONT COVER: The cover image shows students arriving at St. Mary's Hall with Doane Hall and Doane Annex visible in the background around 1900. (Courtesy Eliza G. Doane Archival Library, Doane Academy.)

ON THE BACK COVER: The campus of St. Mary's Hall (later Doane Academy) is seen from the Burlington-Bristol Bridge around 1931. Visible near the left edge of the photograph is the spire of the new St. Mary's Church, the final resting place of St. Mary's Hall founder George Washington Doane. (Courtesy Eliza G. Doane Archival Library, Doane Academy.)

The Campus History Series

St. Mary's Hall and Doane Academy

Jack H. Newman
Foreword by Cynthia McFarland
Introduction by John McGee

ARCADIA
PUBLISHING

Published by Arcadia Publishing
Charleston, South Carolina

Printed in the United States of America

Library of Congress Catalog Card Number: 2011933501

For all general information, please contact Arcadia Publishing:
Telephone 843-853-2070
Fax 843-853-0044
E-mail sales@arcadiapublishing.com
For customer service and orders:
Toll-Free 1-888-313-2665

Visit us on the Internet at www.arcadiapublishing.com

*This book is dedicated to my wife, Tracy, whose love, support,
and constant encouragement is my guiding light.*

CONTENTS

FOREWORD

There was not a worse year to found a private school than 1837. Banks throughout the young United States failed. Currency was devalued. Real estate plummeted.

George Washington Doane, the 37-year-old bishop of New Jersey, had just embarked on selling stock to raise money for St. Mary's Hall, his new school for girls. He had purchased a large house on the Delaware River. He was arranging for teachers, classrooms, and dormitories. However, money became impossibly tight. Friends who had pledged funds gave less. Those who hoped to give could not. Did that discourage him? Not for a moment.

A man with a mission, Doane wanted to show that the education of girls could be as substantive as that of boys. At that time, girls were restricted to botany, sewing, sketching, French, and perhaps the piano. Doane turned that world upside down.

He planned a tough academic curriculum in an atmosphere of comfort, trust, and care in the context of the Episcopal church. Grounded on scripture, tradition, and reason, such a curriculum was the best assurance that his graduates would be intelligently pious in addition to being well educated.

Once the first class arrived in May 1837, Doane officiated at chapel services each morning, noon, and evening whenever he could. He rang the bell at 5:30 a.m. to "rise and shine," and he taught English composition. Here is an eyewitness report:

> He began by asking the girls to write a letter home. Of course any child can write a letter! How glad she is to give vent to her pent-up affections. Then every two weeks, a dozen themes were announced: a proverb, a religious subject; "flowers by the wayside," "a dream," "a pencil," "a needle," "chalk," or "a shocking bad cold." Our compositions must often have wearied him with their dullness, yet he never showed it from the care he took in the analysis and criticism. Even if he had not been the great bishop of his day, his wonderful power as a teacher would have enabled him to wield an influence hardly less mighty.

By such teaching and by such love, he built up St. Mary's Hall until it became the best-known girls' school in the country.

After nearly 200 years, learning, laughter, and love still flourish at this remarkable school. Nothing would make Bishop Doane prouder.

—Cynthia McFarland

ACKNOWLEDGMENTS

My being able to compile and write this book requires that I thank literally dozens if not hundreds of people. From its inception in 1837, the vision, history, and very identity of St. Mary's Hall and Doane Academy have been carried forward by an assembly of caring and diligent people. Over the many decades, the school's educators, administrators, staff, students, and families have not only continued to live Bishop Doane's vision, but have also collected and preserved the story of this school and of those who have walked its hallowed halls. But at the end of the 20th century, all was nearly lost.

In 1999, the school was on the verge of closing its doors, and its archives were left in a heap, ready to be thrown away. The school was rescued from closing by a loan, a dedicated board, and equally dedicated alumni, while the archives were rescued and given new life via the volunteer efforts of Alice "Lollie" Berger Rogers (class of 1961) and Daniel Pugh (class of 2002). In the end, it was their dedicated work to collect, sort, assemble, and catalog so many thousands of scattered documents and photographs that led to the creation of the Eliza G. Doane Archival Library and made this book possible. Unless otherwise noted, all images are courtesy of the Eliza G. Doane Archival Library, Doane Academy.

INTRODUCTION

Organizations that maintain their spirit and vitality from generation to generation have some things in common. The founding mission has to be so visionary and so adaptable that it can evolve over time without altering the organization's basic purpose or compromising its identity. Bishop Doane left his beloved St. Mary's Hall with all of that, but he also somewhat mysteriously incorporated his passion for education and patriotism into the walls and halls of Doane Academy. The school's commitment to leadership and character development as a compliment to academic achievement and its bold new challenge to "Change the World" is simply a 2012 version of Bishop Doane's motto, "Right Onward."

Doane Academy celebrates its past with respect and gratitude as it strategically plans and implements coursework, activities, and expectations that challenge everyone in the school community to make a significant difference in the world. The school has nearly completed the restoration on all three of its historic buildings: Odenheimer Hall (1869), Scarborough Hall (1912), and the Chapel of the Holy Innocents (1847). The plans are well under way to expand enrollment and for the campus to accommodate 300 students over the next 8–10 years (currently at 200 students, prekindergarten–12th grade).

We are pleased, at long last, to have the work of our dedicated former archivist Alice Rogers and current archivist Jack Newman find the light of day in this publication. Anyone who studies these pictures and reads these stories will discover the roots that continue to give life to this extraordinary little school. The school's new identity as Doane Academy speaks loudly and respectfully to the vision and passion of the school's founder, Bishop George Washington Doane. Right Onward . . . Change the World!

—John F. McGee
Headmaster

One

1799–1859

Doane Academy's long, storied history is forever tied to Bishop George Washington Doane. Born in Trenton, New Jersey, on May 27, 1799, Doane was the son of a master carpenter and builder. His insatiable interest in books quickly led him to become a professor of literature, and his deep interest in theology moved him to a life of service to God and community through the Episcopal Church.

In October 1832, while Doane was serving as a rector in Boston, he was called back to the state of his birth to serve as the second bishop of New Jersey. His Boston friends urged him not to go, saying New Jersey was so poor that he would be paid in fruits and vegetables. Doane left against their advice. He chose to live in Burlington, the former colonial capital of New Jersey, situated along the banks of the Delaware River. There, he also became the rector of St. Mary's Church (founded in 1702), which had seen many notable members, including the last royal governor, William Franklin, son of Benjamin Franklin. While he worked at growing his congregation and diocese, this carpenter's son also started thinking about building, both in the material sense and in the sense of an educational visionary.

ST MARY'S HALL, GREEN BANK, BURLINGTON.

UNDER THE SUPERVISION OF THE BISHOP OF NEW JERSEY

Doane had considered opening a school for boys in Burlington. But in late 1836, the building and grounds that had housed the Samuel R. Gummere school for girls was put up for sale. Bishop Doane was inspired to start something new. Doane alerted his friends, including Sen. Garret D. Wall, to his plans, and they helped to arrange the finances to buy the building and property for $16,500 and to place ownership with the bishop. The Gummere School, associated with the Society of Friends, had been similar to most girls' schools of the time, splitting the focus between academics and social and domestic training. Situated regally along the banks of the Delaware River, Doane's school would bring something new to women's education, namely an intense academic education, equal in every way to degree-granting men's schools of the time.

On May 1, 1837, Bishop Doane welcomed 52 young girls to St. Mary's Hall, his new boarding school. The *Philadelphia Inquirer* noted how unusual it was for a religious school to admit students "whatever be their religious birthright, or the profession of their parents." A national financial panic struck just nine days later. Banks failed and closed, and a nationwide depression began. Doane was extremely generous but also a notoriously poor manager of money. The way the bishop had established the school's finances with a low-cost tuition and numerous scholarships meant the school would have to survive mainly on promised endowments, most of which vanished with the onset of the panic and depression. Doane's wife, Eliza Green Doane, offered her $9,500 annual dowry to secure the financial gaps at the school. Eliza Doane truly saved St. Mary's Hall.

As the economy rebounded and opportunity presented itself, Bishop Doane moved forward in 1846 with a plan to open a separate school for boys. Some land and buildings immediately west of where the Burlington-Bristol Bridge now stands were offered to Bishop Doane by Rebecca Chester. After acquiring the property, Doane moved to set up his school. It was opened as Burlington College Preparatory School in November 1846 with the plan to guide the first students through to the newly chartered Burlington College where they would then proceed through degree-granting programs. In his introductory address called "The Ends and Objects of Burlington College," Doane laid out his design for the school to produce men that would be gentlemen, scholars, patriots, and Christians.

BURLINGTON COLLEGE.

CHAPEL OF THE HOLY INNOCENTS

St. Mary's Hall, Burlington, N. J.

From the beginning, Bishop Doane had plans for a chapel on the grounds of St. Mary's Hall, but financial constraints delayed construction. When enough money had been raised, Doane hired John Notman, a noted Scottish architect. On September 25, 1845, the cornerstone was laid, and the Chapel of the Holy Innocents was consecrated on March 25, 1847. Notman's chapel, modeled in part after Stanton, St. John, in Oxfordshire, England, is cited as the first example of Gothic Revival architecture in the United States. The Chapel of the Holy Innocents has seen some changes since its consecration. Minton tiles were added to the floor in 1854. The chapel was extended in 1866 and then attached to Odenheimer Hall in 1868. Through these and other changes, the chapel has retained its original character and has always been the treasured center of the school.

According to archival records, the chapel bell appears to predate the chapel. A bell was originally hung between trees next to the school and was rung by Doane to wake the girls each morning. When the chapel was built, the bell was hoisted to the roof and placed in a wooden tower. The school bell now hangs in the Fisk Portico and peals to announce the start of every school day.

The Bishop's House

About 200 feet west of the chapel stood Riverside, the bishop's house, also designed by famed architect John Notman. This villa was another first for the young United States. It was described as Italian Gothic and had 25 rooms. It was used as the regular residence for the bishops of New Jersey from 1838 into the 1870s and then found use as classroom space, a social club, and visitors' lodgings.

During the 1840s, Ellen Maria Hutchison (seated, with her sister Mary), of Pittsburgh, Pennsylvania, was a student at St. Mary's. In a letter written to her sister Mary dated December 5, 1846, Ellen described her typical day at school: "We get up at half past five O-clock, in the first place we have private devotion in our room, next prayers in the school-room, then our breakfast, immediately after, study hour, then school which lasts until a quarter after two. We have dinner then, and as soon as dinner is over I take my music lesson which lasts half an hour, then I come to writing class until four, then I go to practice for another hour, at six we have tea, as soon as that is over we have study hour, and then prayers, and then we go to bed." (Courtesy Catherine Richert.)

Ellen Hutchison married widowed Pittsburgh lawyer Edwin M. Stanton (pictured here) in 1856, and shortly after, they moved to Washington, DC. In December 1860, Stanton was tapped by outgoing president James Buchanan to replace US attorney general John Floyd. Lincoln kept Stanton on in his cabinet as attorney general until appointing him secretary of war in January 1862. Stanton was at Lincoln's deathbed in 1865 and is credited with saying the famous words, "Now he belongs to the ages," after Lincoln had breathed his last breath. In 1869, Pres. Ulysses S. Grant appointed Stanton to the US Supreme Court. Sadly, Stanton passed away just four days later, leaving behind his widow, Ellen, and their four young children. As told later in this book, Ulysses S. Grant is also connected to St. Mary's Hall. (Courtesy Catherine Richert.)

The courses of study at both St. Mary's Hall and Burlington College were extremely rigorous, and it was demanded that students master the entirety of a subject before they could move on to the next level of study. Courses of instruction included rhetoric, logic, trigonometry, astronomy, chemistry, history, Christian morals and philosophy, Latin, Greek, French, composition, geometry, history of antiquity (Greece and Rome), bookkeeping, and mineralogy.

The caption on the back of this photograph states that the image above is of "Susan MacDonald Nelson and classmates" in front of St. Mary's Hall. Susan MacDonald was a member of the first graduating class of St. Mary's Hall in 1844. She remained active with the school, eventually becoming president of the Society of Graduates and later memorialized when an enclosed brick corridor was named in her honor.

18

St. Mary's Church, Burlington, N. J.

By 1847, St. Mary's Church, situated about a half mile from St. Mary's Hall, was becoming too small to house its growing numbers. Among those attending both of Bishop Doane's services every Sunday were the girls and faculty of St. Mary's Hall. Doane hired John Upton in 1847 to design the new St. Mary's Church. Built next to the old St. Mary's Church, it was consecrated in 1854.

Nancy Stanley, vice principal from 1846 until 1877, taught at Rutgers Institute before joining St. Mary's Hall. One of her more notable contributions is her chairing of the 1874 committee that called for the first reunion of graduates and for the formation of a "society of graduates." The Society of Graduates formed in 1875 and has had annual reunions and tremendous involvement with the school ever since.

Miss Stanley. March 1857.

Elvin K. Smith was "head of the family" (as headmasters were known) at St. Mary's Hall from 1858 through 1878. Smith later wrote of his time at the school in several reminiscences published in the *Ivy Leaves*. In one article, he explained the design of the building that would later be known as Doane Hall: "Every inmate of the Hall must have noticed the peculiar twin-structure of the original school building, with its double staircase and its exactly corresponding rooms on either side, from basement to attic. At the small cost of a brick partition and two entrance doors . . . the building would be easily converted into two ample dwellings. Mr. Gummere told the writer that this was his intention, in case the school should not be successful. The bishop's purchase preserved it for its original purpose, under better auspices."

A student of interest from this pre–Civil War era is Margaret G. Howell. Sister-in-law of US senator and then Confederate president Jefferson Davis (right), Howell attended St. Mary's beginning in 1858. Davis is listed as her guardian in the school registers. In the days leading up to the war, Howell predicted that she would be "one of the royal ladies" when a new monarchy was set up at Richmond.

Ada Winans, pictured here around 1860, graduated from the school in 1853 and taught music at St. Mary's Hall from 1856 to 1861 when she left to pursue a career as an opera singer. She was in Florence, Italy, in early 1864 when she met Prince Petr Troubetzky, of Russia, a cousin of the ruling Romanov family. They later married, making Ada the princess from St. Mary's Hall.

On April 27, 1859, after a brief illness, George Washington Doane passed away at Riverside. Four days later, a funeral procession estimated at 3,000 people, including the governor of New Jersey and other notables, left from Riverside, proceeded along the riverbank, then down Wood Street, to new St. Mary's Church, where the late bishop was laid to rest in the churchyard. During his nearly 26 years as bishop, he had been an agent of great change. Besides leading a revolution in women's education, Doane had also founded Burlington College for boys and had expanded the reach of the Episcopal Church in New Jersey from 27 parishes upon his arrival in 1833 to 85 parishes by 1859.

Two

1859–1890s

Immediately after the bishop's passing, memorials were discussed. Besides a scholarship in his name, it was quickly decided that there would also be a memorial window placed in the south end of the chapel. Owen Dormeus was commissioned to design the window. In the center panel below the harp are the bishop's coat of arms and his personal motto, "Right Onward," which later became the school's motto as well.

William Henry Odenheimer succeeded Bishop Doane as bishop of New Jersey. His diligent work helped to alleviate fears expressed by many that St. Mary's and Burlington College could not go on without Doane at the helm. Odenheimer lived at Riverside and acted as president of the school. He passed away at Riverside on August 14, 1879.

With the outbreak of the Civil War in April 1861, many of the dozens of Southern girls at St. Mary's Hall were called home, often with agents of the school escorting them "to the lines." Susan Gooding Becton, of North Carolina, was one of several exceptions. She stayed on and is pictured here in her 1862 graduation portrait.

Many feared that as Southern girls went home at the onset of war, the school would falter and fail, but as Northern industry ramped up to meet the demands of war, many businessmen suddenly found that they now had the financial means to send their children to better schools. Pictured at right is Virginia Wolff (class of 1862), of Pottsville, Pennsylvania. At the outbreak of the war, there were 190 students enrolled at St. Mary's Hall. When the fall 1861 term began, that number dwindled to 127. With the influx of new Northern students, the numbers quickly rebounded with 153 students in the fall of 1862, a total of 186 in 1863, and 194 by 1864. The numbers continued to grow through the end of the war and into the 1870s.

Pictured are members of the class of 1865, the largest graduating class up to that time.

In early 1864, Ulysses S. Grant was looking for a home for his family far from the fighting. At the suggestion of a friend, Grant chose Burlington. Grant moved his family into a house at 309 Wood Street and sent sons Fred and Ulysses to Burlington College while his daughter Millie was tutored by the instructors of St. Mary's Hall. During a personal tour of St. Mary's Hall, Grant happened to open a door where a few girls were sitting in solemn silence. These were Southern girls who had actually refused to entertain the Northern general and had locked themselves away. Grant mistakenly assumed that these girls were being disciplined for something. He apologized for intruding upon girls who were being punished and quickly closed the door. The Southern girls were little amused by his comments.

ST. MARY'S HALL.
BURLINGTON N.J.

The school was continually expanding its physical plant. By the 1860s, as pictured here, the school had expanded east with the building of a new wing (later known as Doane Annex) on the land where Mrs. Lippincott's cottage had previously stood. It was during this time that the school had also purchased a farm on adjacent property to the west. As a result, a mortgage bond of the time refers to the collective property as "St. Mary's Hall, Riverside, Burlington College and Farm." U.S. Grant's sons were a major distraction for the girls of St. Mary's Hall during this time, and when Fred and Ulysses would drive in the cows from the farm each night, the girls would often "make up excuses to get out and see them."

27

George Hobart Doane (born in 1830), son of the bishop and Eliza Doane, was among the first graduates of Burlington College, the boys' school founded by his father. He went on to graduate from Jefferson Medical School before having a calling to religious service—in the Catholic Church. Father and son had a falling-out for a few years but reconciled before Bishop Doane's death. George H. Doane died in 1905.

William Croswell Doane, another of Bishop Doane's sons, was also a graduate of Burlington College. Born in 1832, he followed his father's lead and dedicated himself to the Episcopal Church. He served for over 60 years, including 44 years as the first bishop of Albany, New York. He also wrote a detailed four-volume biography of his father, which was astoundingly published just one year after George W. Doane's death.

In 1868, with the school growing consistently, ground was broken on a new building, much later to be named Odenheimer Hall. A three-and-a-half-story brick structure, it was attached to the south end of the chapel extension. In its original internal configuration, the basement was used as the kitchen and dining hall. The first floor had a library just outside of the chapel, and just past the entrance hall was a wide-open study hall and auditorium with a row of iron pillars running down the center of the hall, breaking up the open space. The second and third floors were at first open dormitories with rows of beds and little or no privacy. Later, seven-foot-high partitions were put in to give the girls a modicum of privacy. By the turn of the century, the second and third floors were converted into fully separated rooms with completed walls. Today, the dormitories and study hall have been converted to offices, classrooms, libraries, and art studios.

Lacking the novelty of St. Mary's Hall, Burlington College, the boys' school, never found a solid footing and continuously ran up debts that were then covered by the profits of St. Mary's Hall. In 1870, the combined board of both schools, known as the Trustees of Burlington College, decided that the college would have to succeed or fail on its own. The school soldiered on through the early 1870s but was dealt a deathblow by the epidemics that struck Burlington in the mid-1870s. Burlington College, already in deep debt when illness struck the town, saw many students withdrawn out of fear for their lives. Enrollment fell drastically, and the institution closed in November 1877. Interestingly though, St. Mary's Hall continued to operate under the supervision of the Trustees of Burlington College until a charter and name change in 2008.

Class of 1877

The Burlington area and St. Mary's Hall were struck by typhoid in December 1874, and the disease took the lives of three students. Scarlet fever took the life of another student the following April, and diphtheria took yet another life in early 1876. Through these trials, the school survived with the help of new mortgage bonds as well as the determination of the board, faculty, and families of St. Mary's Hall.

The dwindling enrollment and financial hardship brought on by the illnesses eventually led to the resignation of Elvin K. Smith as head of the family, or principal, in 1878. His replacement was the Reverend J. Leighton McKim (shown here), who spent most of his nine-year tenure restoring enrollment at the school and finding ways to retire the nearly $60,000 in total debt (the equivalent of over $1.3 million today).

31

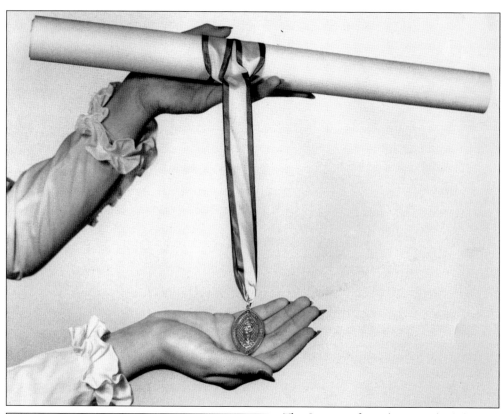

The Society of Graduates, which had been meeting annually since 1875, adopted the silver medal above as their badge in 1880. One of these medals hung on a blue-and-white ribbon has been given to every graduate of the school ever since and, according to tradition, is to be returned to the school upon the graduate's death to then be given to a new honorary member of the society.

Through the 19th century, girls were sent from far and wide to attend St. Mary's Hall. The school's registers show students sent from as far away as the Florida Keys, San Francisco, and a few girls actually came from outside of the United States. These early students traveled to and from school via stagecoach, train, or boat. This illustration by J. Collins dates from 1883.

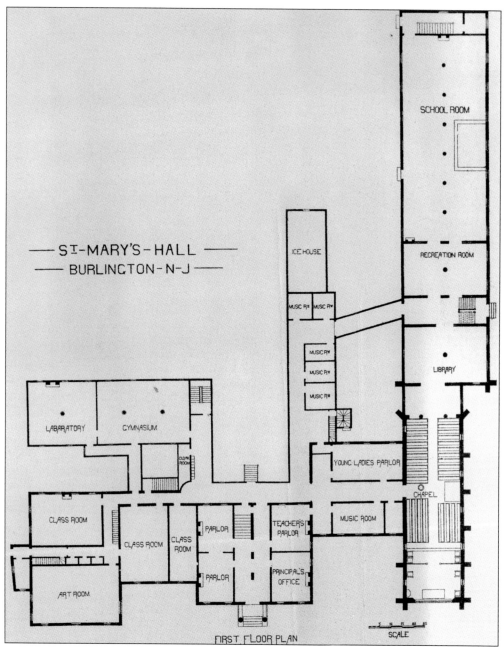

St-MARY'S-HALL
BURLINGTON-N-J

ICE HOUSE

SCHOOL ROOM

RECREATION ROOM

MUSIC R⁴ MUSIC R⁴

MUSIC R⁴

MUSIC R⁴

LIBRARY

MUSIC R⁴

LABARATORY GYMNASIUM

CLOAK ROOM

YOUNG LADIES PARLOR

CHAPEL

CLASS ROOM

MUSIC ROOM

PARLOR

CLASS ROOM CLASS ROOM

TEACHERS PARLOR

ART ROOM

PARLOR

PRINCIPAL'S OFFICE

FIRST FLOOR PLAN

SCALE

This is the floor plan of the school at the time of its 50th anniversary in 1887, and it vividly displays the growth of the school. The original building is represented by the small square at the bottom center. The square structure to its right, later known as the Chapel Annex, was actually added in the years before the construction of the chapel. To the left and rear of the main building is the structure housing the laboratory and gymnasium, which was described as a "wooden pioneer" edifice. The building in the lower left, known as Doane Annex, was added after the demolition of Mrs. Lippincott's cottage. The building now known as Odenheimer Hall extends along the right of the image and shows its original open floor plan.

The 1890s brought new vigor to the school. All debts were paid off, and two scholarships were set up with the newfound surplus. There were even stirrings of adding a St. Mary's College where Burlington College had once operated. The girls of the hall were also finding a new surplus of time, as the demanding schedules of old gave way and afforded chances for diversion. In the early days, the girls began their day at 5:30 a.m. and generally had no real free time to themselves six days per week. On Sundays, the girls may have been allowed to go into Burlington City—as long as they were chaperoned. The girls of the 1890s were enjoying tennis, croquet, and horseback riding alongside the river, that "cruising ground of kings," as Bishop Doane had called it.

Three

1890s–1912

The interior of the Chapel of the Holy Innocents is pictured just after the installation of a newer chapel organ. The previous organ dated from about 1860, and it was failing by 1890. The replacement organ was larger and deeper than the original, and it quickly became obvious that an alcove extension would need to be constructed.

Ivy Leaves.

" Right Onward."

OCTOBER, 1895.	ST. MARY'S HALL, BURLINGTON, N. J.	VOL. IV. No. 6

In 1892, the faculty and students began a new venture, a regular publication they named the *Ivy Leaves*. The name is an homage to the ivy that covered the school buildings, which had also been symbolically used in many graduation and dedication ceremonies at the hall. As part of the graduation ceremonies through at least the 1890s, each girl had three ivy leaves plucked from the chapel wall and pinned on her gown. The *Ivy Leaves*, published to this day, has been enjoyed in several forms over the years. There has been a graduate edition, a student edition, and a literary edition called the *Ivy Voice*.

A typical double-occupancy dorm room appears above as it looked in 1898. Obviously, teenagers liked to decorate their rooms back then, just as much as they do today. The wall on the left does not extend to the ceiling. Privacy was still hard to come by, even in one's own dorm room. Also, "house mothers" continually monitored the order (or disorder) of each dorm room.

Although St. Mary's Hall was considered progressive from its inception, it still reflected some of the established norms of its time. Here, some students are attending a cooking class in the "new" kitchen in the basement of Odenheimer Hall. The future husbands of these students would of course expect them to be knowledgeable of at least some things domestic.

With the turn of the 19th century came new leadership in the form of the Reverend and Mrs. John Fearnley. Beulah Fearnley, the principal, had previously taught at the school, starting in 1890, and was one of the founders of *Ivy Leaves*. Her husband served as chaplain of the school. From 1900 until 1925, Beulah Fearnley led the school through numerous changes and some improvements while her husband was the ever-present spiritual guide for the hall. The old Burlington College property was finally sold to the Thomas Devlin Manufacturing Company in 1902, but other land and properties were purchased during these years. A new heating plant was installed, electricity found its way into the school, and new construction expanded the campus facilities. Beulah also helped to grow the Society of Graduates by suggesting the founding of regional chapters.

The chapel is shown shortly after the addition of the organ alcove. This pushing out of part of the western wall altered Notman's original footprint of the building but restored the original interior sight lines. The "new" organ of the 1890s seems to actually have been a well-worn old instrument, which needed to be completely replaced by 1900. The Society of Graduates donated most of the funds for this undertaking, and a well-refurbished Jardine organ was installed in the existing casework in May 1900. Also in the early 1900s, the altar and the screen behind it were restored and enhanced through the gifts of graduates of the school, and gas lighting stands were converted to electric lighting by 1915.

As early as the 1840s, the girls were putting on musical rehearsals as well as soirees and other performances. By the late 1800s, they were creating their own tableaus, which were very popular through at least the 1920s. A tableau is defined as a group of motionless actors representing a scene or several scenes from history or a story from literature.

The students also performed numerous pageants, which were closer to the plays of today. Most of these pageants were held outside on the grounds behind Riverside. This image, taken in 1923, represents characters from three stories, which are, from left to right, *Beauty and the Beast*, *Sleeping Beauty*, and *Puss in Boots*.

These images represent just a couple of the dozens of pageants and tableaus that the girls of St. Mary's Hall put on in the early 1900s. Of course, the school was still an all-girls-only institution at the time, so girls played all of the roles, male and female, a kind of reversal of the Shakespearean tradition. The pageants became an event in the area and often drew hundreds of people from Burlington City and beyond. These shows became so well known as to be featured in articles in newspapers like the *New York Herald*, the *Philadelphia Sunday News*, and *Burlington County's Daily Enterprise*. In its June 1, 1902, edition, the *Sunday News* notes that the school once again "will be transformed into a fairyland." The two photographs chosen here are of the stories of *Cinderella* and *Coming through the Rye*.

Pictured is one of the many music rooms of the early 1900s. This one was most likely in the Chapel Annex. Piano playing was a national pastime in this era, reflected in a contemporary inventory of St. Mary's Hall, which counts six grand pianos and three upright pianos among its possessions. The school continues to this day to value and promote a rich musical program.

As years passed and other schools caught up with the advances of St. Mary's Hall, the number of boarding students dropped. As parents found similar schools opening closer to home, they chose not to send their girls to far-off boarding schools. By the end of the 19th century, most students came from New Jersey, Pennsylvania, and New York. In 1906, only nine students came from beyond those three states.

One of the magnetic and ever-changing features of the school is the Delaware River, which runs directly in front of the campus. Pictured viewing an ice flow (well before the construction of the Burlington-Bristol Bridge) are students Naomi Long and Frances Livingston, both members of the class of 1908.

Among the members of the class of 1909 was Anne Zollars (unidentified here), who went on to serve with the Red Cross Motor Service Corps, moving supplies to destitute French citizens in the aftermath of World War I. Zollars was awarded two service medals by the French government before dying of Spanish influenza in Paris in 1919. Her classmates memorialized her with a plaque that now hangs in the chapel.

CLASS of 1909

The Episcopal Diocese of New Jersey had grown to such an extent that it needed to be divided by 1874. John Scarborough was elected the new bishop of the southern portion in 1875, a position that he held until his death in 1914. During his 40 years as bishop, although he chose not to live at Riverside or even in Burlington City, he was a constant presence at the school. As presiding officer of the board of trustees and the executive committee for over 39 years, he guided much of what occurred at St. Mary's Hall. His kind, gentle demeanor and ability to remember everyone by name after just one meeting endeared him to all at the school and beyond. To many, he was known as the "Merry Bishop."

As Bishop Scarborough (1831–1914) moved toward the end of his tenure and his life, he made known his wish to see "a fine dining hall and gymnasium as part of the equipment of St. Mary's Hall." A building fund was started, and the "pioneer" structures housing the old laboratory and gymnasium were pulled down in anticipation of the new structure to rise in its place.

William Hewitt, architect and member of the board, created and gave his plans for this new building to the school, and Bishop Scarborough donated much of the funds needed for construction to begin. The cornerstone was laid May 31, 1911, and this new building was dedicated as Scarborough Hall on May 1, 1912, the school's 75th anniversary.

Four

1912–1937

Scarborough Hall had everything that its namesake had asked for and more. On the first floor was (and still is) a beautifully paneled dining hall with beamed ceilings and a large hearth. On the second floor were a number of boarding rooms. Shown here is the gymnasium, which was located on the third floor and is now used as an auditorium.

The 75th anniversary of the founding of St. Mary's Hall was marked with celebrations and more changes to the school. The graduates returned in force for this anniversary, as is demonstrated in this photograph. After a historic sermon in the chapel recalling Bishop Doane's vision for the school, the very first luncheon was held in the newly dedicated (but unfinished) Scarborough Hall. During this occasion, it was announced that two other buildings of the school would be formally named: the original building, now to be known as Doane Hall, and the 1868 building as Odenheimer Hall. After the luncheon, the girls of the school treated the faculty and guests to their May Day pageant and winding of the maypoles.

During the 75th anniversary celebration, it was announced that the New York chapter of the Society of Graduates had raised enough funds to construct a cloister that would offer an enclosed connection between the new Scarborough Hall and the older buildings. Nelson Corridor, named in honor of Susan MacDonald Nelson, was completed within the year.

THIS CORRIDOR
GIVEN BY THE
NEW YORK CHAPTER
OF THE
DAUGHTERS OF ST. MARY'S HALL
IN MEMORY OF
SUSAN McDONALD NELSON
1829 – 1910
A MEMBER OF THE
FIRST GRADUATING CLASS 1844

Beulah Fearnley, seen here with some students on the frozen Delaware River, oversaw a great expansion of athletics and the activities available to the girls of the school, including ice-skating. The girls now had among their choices basketball, field hockey, archery, and canoeing. As female participation in sports was still shunned in most corners, St. Mary's Hall offered a progressive alternative.

While St. Mary's Hall stood within the boundaries of Burlington City, girls of the hall had rarely been permitted to partake in the shopping and entertainment available there until the time of Beulah Fearnley. In this era, the city saw a bit of a renaissance, as people from the Philadelphia region often came to Burlington City and its adjacent township as places to vacation in the summer. Burlington Township had Sylvan Lakes, a place where people could rent cabins and enjoy canoeing, fishing, swimming, and nightly activities at a music hall. Burlington City offered shopping, a movie house, an opera house, and an amusement park on Burlington Island. The amusement park named Island Beach Park had picnic grounds, live entertainment, many rides, and a roller coaster called the Grey Hound. Burlington Island is seen in the distance in this photograph taken from the Green Bank in front of St. Mary's.

The 1920s are often referred to as the Roaring Twenties, or the Flapper Era. It was a time when cultural norms were shifting, women were becoming more liberated, and when the United States was experiencing an unprecedented financial boom. The girls of St. Mary's Hall changed with these times. Gone were the drab clothes, the bound-up long hair, and the meek behavior of old. And yet, at this same time of the awakening of women across the country, St. Mary's Hall was sliding backward, away from its former leadership in women's education, and was becoming more of a finishing school. Strangely, at the end of her 25 years at the school, Beulah Fearnley seemed almost proud of the fact that out of the over 400 girls who graduated during her tenure, only 33 girls went on to college.

Riverside was little used after the bishops of New Jersey had removed themselves from Burlington. For several years, it was rented out to families and then to some social clubs of Burlington before being damaged by fire. By the 1920s, it was nearly in ruins when the trustees finally had it restored and electricity added. The restoration was done by architect Henry A. Brown, husband of 1905 graduate Alice English.

Fairholm, located opposite the school across Ellis Street, was acquired in 1918 from William D. Hewitt, trustee and the architect of Scarborough Hall. He was also a graduate of Burlington College. The structure was a Colonial-era building that needed some restoration but ended up serving many purposes over the coming decades. It was used as the headmaster's house, as a boardinghouse, for classroom space, and for formal receptions.

Succeeding Bishop Scarborough in 1915 was Rev. Paul Matthews. The new bishop sent his daughter Harriet to the school in the fall of 1922. Sadly, she became ill over the Christmas break and died in New York City on December 29, 1922. Bishop Matthews set up a memorial endowment in her name at St. Mary's Hall with an initial gift of $50,000, equal to over $600,000 today.

The bishop did not often visit the school, but when he did, the girls were usually left in pain "from laughing too much." They would invite him to dance with them in the gymnasium where he would, to their joy, demonstrate the Virginia reel. Bishop Matthews resigned as bishop in 1937 at age 70 but became a regular visitor and generous donor to the school until his death in 1954.

In 1926, St. Mary's Hall absorbed the students of Ruth Hall of Asbury Park, a first-through-sixth-grade girls' school. A recently acquired Victorian building, previously known as Maison Rouge (French for "Red House"), was converted to house the new lower school and was renamed Ruth Hall. It was now possible for a young girl to attend St. Mary's Hall from first through 12th grade.

The grounds of St. Mary's Hall were extensive in the 1920s, including this field located southeast of the intersection of Ellis and Pearl Streets. This same field also doubled as a riding ring for the girls and their horses. The land was sold to Burlington City in 1955 and is now the site of the Elias Boudinot Elementary School.

When the Fearnleys retired to travel the world in 1925, the board decided to bring the school's focus back to faith and academics. To this end, they placed the Sisters of the Transfiguration, an Anglican order founded by Bishop Matthews's sister, in charge of the school, with Sr. Edith Constance, the bishop's niece, as its new principal.

Over the next two years, the Sisters of the Transfiguration reorganized much of the school and effectively made preparing the girls for college the primary focus. Gone were much of the free time and leisure activities of the Fearnley era. In came strict new rules and codes—and for the first time in the school's history, uniforms.

Taking care of boarding students in the late 1920s was Ruth Davis, mother of future film star Bette Davis, pictured here. Bette later stated in her autobiography that her mother was able to pay for her acting lessons in New York with the money she earned at St. Mary's. Bette Davis kept correspondence with the school through at least 1938 when she last bought a full-page advertisement in the yearbook.

Sr. Edith Constance and the Sisters of the Transfiguration resigned in 1927, citing financial problems within the school as their reason for leaving. It is known that the Society of Graduates and some parents were not happy with the strict religious administration, and this may have contributed to the move. Seen here are the girls of the upper and lower school enjoying a field day together.

The incorporation of a lower school is evident in this photograph from a pageant of the era, but something else may be revealed here. That mule just may be a boy. By the 1930s, the school was admitting several young, male day students up through grade eight, although they did not advertise this fact.

In 1927, the trustees turned to a lay principal for the first time since the 1880s and chose Ethel M. Spurr. She moved the school toward higher academic standards with the goal of being accredited by the Middle States Association of Secondary Schools and Colleges, an accreditation the school still holds. During her tenure, St. Mary's Hall was successful at balancing stronger scholastics with physical education and social activities.

In 1927, businessmen of Burlington, New Jersey, and Bristol, Pennsylvania, discussed the possibility of replacing the centuries-old ferry between the towns with a bridge. The Burlington-Bristol Bridge Company was formed, and after a brief plan to run the bridge across Burlington Island, a site adjacent to St. Mary's Hall was selected. After some negotiation, the school's board transferred some land and riparian rights to the company in exchange for $6,000, some paint on the campus buildings, and an iron fence to separate the school grounds from the bridge. The school later decided to take more cash instead of the paint and fencing. The bridge opened on May 1, 1931, after just 13 months of construction. The result for the school was an increase in day students coming in from Pennsylvania and some financial relief from the effects of the Great Depression.

Edith Weller, who had started at the school as a teacher of mathematics in the 1920s, had moved up to vice principal and then finally to principal in 1933. In an interesting experiment she instituted during her tenure, tuition became graduated based upon a student's grades. A yearly tuition was now between $700 and $900 per year, dependent upon grades.

St. Mary's Hall weathered the Great Depression with moderate difficulties. The lack of a proper endowment led to the need to reduce faculty salaries. The families of the school and students banded together to help in these hard times. Students and parents helped physically and financially with the landscaping, gardening, painting, and even the installation of a new kitchen in the basement of Scarborough Hall.

In 1936, the Works Projects Administration, which had been surveying historic American structures, came to St. Mary's Hall and more specifically to Riverside, the bishop's house. Over the course of six months, engineers, architects, and draftsmen documented every aspect of the historic Italianate structure. Several photographs and 44 highly detailed architectural drawings were made of the interior and exterior. Among the noted features were the uniquely paneled library with its Gothic, arched coiling and the cast-iron balustrade of the main stairway to be found in no other structure anywhere. These studies were deposited in the Library of Congress and are available for viewing online at www. loc.gov/pictures/item/nj0313.

Five

1937–1955

At a diocesan convention in 1834, George Washington Doane said, "There is nothing in so great demand among us as a good education, and there is nothing so scarce." On the 100th anniversary of the opening of his first school to remedy that problem, people gathered from across the nation to mark the many accomplishments of his little school on the Delaware River.

Centennial Celebration
St. Mary's Hall
1837-1937

May the Twenty-seventh to May the Thirtieth

Founder's Day, Thursday, May Twenty-seventh

10:30 A.M. . . . . Chapel Service
Preacher: THE RT. REV. JOHN C. WARD, D.D., Bishop of Erie
Followed by crowning of portrait
1:00 P.M. Luncheon
4:00 P.M. . . . . Alumnæ Review
8:30 P.M. Reception

Centennial Day, Friday, May Twenty-eighth

11:00 A.M. . . . . Service at St. Mary's Church
Preacher: THE MOST REV. JAMES DeW. PERRY, D.D., Presiding Bishop
1:00 P.M. Luncheon
2:00 P.M. . . . . Address
"The Forgotten Woman in the History of St. Mary's Hall"
THE REV. WALTER H. STOWE
Historiographer of the Diocese of New Jersey
3:00 P.M. . . . . Pageant
THE PUPILS OF THE SCHOOL

St. Mary's Day, Saturday, May Twenty-ninth

10:30 A.M. . . . . Educational Program
Speakers:
DR. MARY E. WOOLLEY, President, Mount Holyoke College
DR. WILLIAM ALFRED EDDY, President, Hobart College
1:00 P.M. Luncheon
2:30 P.M. Pageant
THE PUPILS OF THE SCHOOL
5:00 P.M. . . . . Tea at Riverside

Memorial Day, Sunday, May Thirtieth

11:00 A.M. . . . . Service at St. Mary's Church
Preacher: THE RT. REV. PHILIP COOK, D.D., President of the National Council

Followed by Memorial Service at Bishop Doane's Grave

THE RT. REV. PAUL MATTHEWS, D.D., Bishop of New Jersey

The centennial of the school was marked in 1937 with a four-day celebration beginning on May 27, Founder's Day, also Bishop Doane's birthday. Over the course of that extended weekend, hundreds of alumni, parents, faculty of the past and present, and friends of the school marked the occasion with addresses, a theatrical review, a procession to Bishop Doane's grave, and a grand pageant illustrating the history of Burlington from the time before European settlers arrived up until 1937. The newly installed Bishop Wallace Gardner was drafted into the pageant to portray Bishop Odenheimer and is famously quoted as saying, "What a man will do for a woman," as he dressed for his role. While the students surely enjoyed the celebrations, it must be noted that not all was fun and games. An internal memo stated that the girls were to be studying in their rooms after dinner on Friday and Sunday.

The summer of 1940 saw the arrival of new principal Florence Newbold, who previously had been the executive director of the Girl Scouts of Philadelphia. It is noted that during her 12 years as principal, student government grew, an honor code was established, and the Service League, which attended to issues from community service to "world outlook," was formed.

In the 1930s, the school had acquired a bus that made three separate runs each day to bring day students to the school. With the outbreak of World War II and in keeping with the patriotic foundations of the school, the bus was loaned to the Fleetwings Company of Bristol to help them transport workers and support the war effort. Most students from Bristol now "walked the bridge" to school.

During the 1930s, the students of Ruth Hall were brought into the main buildings of St. Mary's Hall for both classes and boarding. The young students now slept in the open dormitory on the third floor of Doane Hall. Ruth Hall was repurposed and was now home to the senior class. At this time, the building was renamed Senior House.

During World War II, the school rationed its resources and spent money only on maintenance they deemed necessary to the operation of the school. This belt-tightening left no budget for Senior House, leading to its quick decline. By 1945, there were structural issues, and the trustees decided to raze the "obsolete building." The area where Senior House stood is now part of the school's main soccer field.

Shortly after the attack on Pearl Harbor and the United States' official entry into World War II, the area west of the Burlington-Bristol Bridge, which had once housed the boys and buildings of Burlington College, was developed by the Defence Plant Corporation. An aluminum factory was constructed on the site; for the most part, it manufactured aircraft skins and parts for the Army Air Corps. As a result, the last of the Burlington College structures were razed at this time. The board of trustees was concerned about what impact this factory might have on the school in increased noise and overall appearance but soon found that existing trees and the bridge acted as an effective screen.

With the war came shortages and rationing coupons. Patricia Van Horn Lix (class of 1945) visited the school in 2010 and told a class of students about how faculty collected student ration books and used them according to need during the war. Lix said she was still upset at how her one and only shoe coupon was used for "church shoes" when she had instead wanted new athletic shoes.

Through World War II, St. Mary's Hall was host to about a dozen girls who were sent from England to avoid the bombing raids and overall threats of war. Most of the tuitions of these girls were covered by scholarships and sponsorships from local families. This experience broadened understanding between cultures and fostered some international friendships that lasted a lifetime.

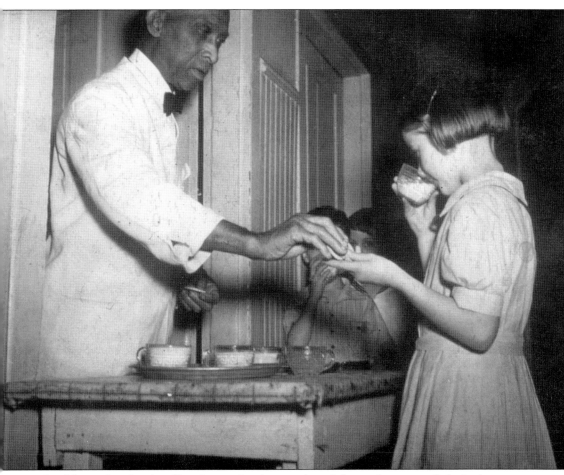

Much of the male school staff and some faculty members left to volunteer to fight in the war. William "Willie" Huggs, the butler who had been with the school since before 1900, was one of the few men who remained behind. Huggs took on additional duties but was also eagerly aided by the students of the school. According to Nancy MacFarland Wismer (class of 1943), Willie was "almost as important as the chapel." Willie, she said, was "always sporting a warm smile, and welcomed every girl to school each morning." He is remembered for his over 50 years of dedication to the school through the Huggs Family, one of several school peer groups comprised of teachers and students from several grades, named in honor of esteemed people from the school's history. Huggs passed away in 1944.

Academically, the school continued to blossom, as evidenced by this quote from a 1940s report of the Middle States Association: "The curriculum and courses of study are superior, as are the plans for their development. Organization and procedure are superior. The amount of offering is generous. There is considerable latitude of choice for the older students. The content of the courses is better than satisfactory, superior in many ways."

While the older girls were contemplating offers from Cornell, the University of Pennsylvania, Swarthmore, and others, they also eagerly anticipated social events at St. Mary's Hall. In preparation, the study hall (pictured in the photograph above) would be cleared and decorated, as the school often hosted dances with guests from Bordentown Military Institute and Valley Forge Military Academy.

The *Christmas Mystery* is a tradition at Doane Academy that has its origins in the earliest days of the school. From 1837 until the 1870s, the girls were required to stay at the hall through the Christmas season. Early school catalogs state, "They come to us as to a father and a mother . . . we have our Christmas, too; and must have our children, keep it, with us. . . . We have no notion to be theirs for work and not for play. . . . They must be ours . . . for holidays and holy days. Otherwise, we are of little use to them." The girls created entertainments for their school family, including one that later grew into a three-part tableau, which by 1930, was the scripted play well known and performed every Christmas season at Doane Academy. Seen here is the *Christmas Mystery* performance of 1945.

The Delaware River has offered inspiration and opportunity to those at this campus since 1837. Bishop Doane and many of those who came after have been inspired to write about the river, what they saw there, and the symbolism of flowing water. The river also offers recreation, challenges to physical limits, and character-building opportunities. The school continues to utilize the river for all of these benefits and more.

While seated in his library at Riverside and gazing out on the Delaware River, George Washington Doane was inspired to write, among his volumes of work, the hymns "Fling Out the Banner" and "Softly Now the Light of Day," two works still sung and recited regularly at the school and beyond. At left, graduates pose outside of the library of Riverside.

When a new library was opened in the Doane Annex, the old library outside of the chapel was repurposed. A wall separating the old space into two rooms was constructed. The eastern room came to be known as the ante-chapel while the western room, seen here, was made into another music instruction room. This room is currently used as the headmaster's office.

Students of the lower school were becoming more involved with service activities. In fact, by 1950, lower school students regularly contributed to projects with the Junior Red Cross and the Service League. Of course, there was still time for fun for the children. Above, students are engaged in an exercise known as "musical shorthand," which they later demonstrated at a school assembly.

The Glee Club was growing in skill and popularity in the late 1940s and early 1950s. Besides performing at regular school concerts, they were now also singing at the Christmas feast and commencement and were being requested to perform at Pennington, Haverford, and the Peddie Schools. It was also noted that they "have recorded quite a few" songs.

The St. Mary's field hockey team had been competing regionally since 1931 and generated enough interest within the school to support a junior varsity team as well. By the mid-1940s, even more girls wanted to participate, so it was decided to create two competing teams within the school, the Whites and the Blues. A rivalry grew between the squads and lasted into the 1960s.

The added chores that the girls attended to during the war years did not fade away in the postwar era. It was now fully expected that much of the maintenance of the school property would be eagerly attended to by the students, and they did not disappoint. How many passersby must have been surprised to see students of this old boarding school happily painting fences or working with intensity in the garden.

Fairholm is seen in the interior photograph as it looked after being converted back to a residence. In its prior incarnations, it was used as a chemistry lab, for classrooms, boarding space, and even an infirmary. In this latest configuration (from about 1950), it was used as the headmistress/headmaster's house.

The 1952–1953 school year marked a turning point in the school's history. Boarding students at this point had dwindled to about 40, leading to the decision that the option be phased out altogether. The girls that were in 9th through 12th grades would be allowed to continue as boarders until their graduation, but the younger boarders would not be readmitted the following year. Another change that came in this year was the decision to actively recruit boys for the lower school. At first, the school would only admit boys up to third grade. Within four years, though, the school allowed boys to attend until their completion of eighth grade. Seen here are some of the boarding students enjoying leisure time on Nelson Porch and the grounds beyond.

With the transition to a coeducational day school, enrollment increased dramatically, especially in the lower school, which saw an increase from 40 students in 1953 to 94 students the following year. Around the time of this growth spurt, the lower school began electing its own student council and started its own school newspaper.

The students of St. Mary's always have been interested in community activities, as can be seen in the Burlington City Halloween parade. The school's float entry is seen on the flatbed truck, while the girls of the school trail behind in their St. Mary's Marching Unit. According to the writings of headmaster Florence Newbold, the school was often ranked first by the judges.

Florence Newbold (sitting behind the table), headmaster since 1940, departed at the close of the 1952 school year. Her impact can be noted in this quote from the class of 1952: "Feel assured that when, as alumnae, we retrace our steps through the halls, she will be foremost in our thoughts. For we will never say good-bye to the things that she taught and the thoughts that she guided."

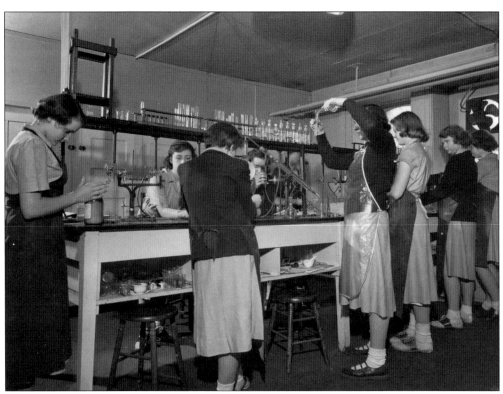

As the Cold War and race to space heated up, schools across the nation began to realize that the emphasis on reading, writing, and arithmetic was not good enough anymore. They now needed to build science and engineering programs. St. Mary's Hall, which had had chemistry, astronomy, and other science programs since the 1840s, was prepared well ahead of the change in national education standards.

In 1946, the school planned a Forward Festival to raise money for their Reconstruction and Advance Fund to aid with the reconstruction of churches and schools across war-torn Europe. By the 1950s, this festival changed focus and became an annual fundraiser for improvements at St. Mary's Hall. The new Spring Festival had a $1 admittance fee, which included all events, except the dinner and auction in the dining hall. Parents, grandparents, and many others came to shop the student booths where students sold their art and craft work among a variety of other items. The day included a Blue vs. White field hockey game, a father-and-daughter baseball game, a maypole dance, tumbling demonstrations, and Glee Club performances.

In 1954, in part to help cover the extensive costs of converting the boarding rooms to classroom space, the board of trustees had taken out a $45,000 mortgage on the property. Apparently, this move upset the new bishop, Rev. Alfred L. Banyard, to the extent that he requested that the church dissolve ties to the school. In a letter to parents, principal Elsie Flounders explained that because the diocese was unable to provide substantial assistance, it was agreed that an independent status would better serve the school, opening new avenues and opportunities. Flounders assured all that the change would not affect the school's programs or its emphasis on spiritual values. The Episcopal tradition, she said, "will be preserved without change." The school retained its Episcopal traditions and eventually established a renewed yet more informal relationship with the Episcopal Church.

Frances Taylor, seen here in Doane Hall, was a fixture at the school for 30 years beginning in 1931. The school's only teacher of Latin during that period, she was also dean of girls. The Bishop's Feast was one tradition that she was sad to see end during her tenure. She told of how Bishop Gardner would come to the school and after dinner would read *A Christmas Carol* by Charles Dickens.

The class of 1960 dedicated their yearbook to Taylor with, *"In freta dum fluvi current, dum montibus umbrae, lustrabunt convexa polus dum sidera pascet, semper honos, nomenque tuum laudesque manebunt!"* ("As long as the rivers run through the valleys, as long as the clouds pass over the mountains, as long as the stars shine in the heavens, always shall thy name, thy honor, and thy praises abide!"), a quote from Virgil's *Aeneid*.

In 1954, St. Mary's Hall joined in a program created to foster relationships and understanding across the globe. Art for World Friendship sought to build on the postwar ideas for constructing a peaceful world. In this program, children sent their artwork overseas and in turn received one from a child of the same age from another country.

In the October 1958 *Ivy Leaves*, new students were asked what their first impressions of the school were. Among the answers were, "The hominess of the school impressed me," "I noticed the politeness of the girls and the kind thoughtful teachers," "I was glad to see such small classes. Last year I was in a class of 46," and "I thought wearing uniforms seemed strange." Current comments are very similar.

Six

1955–1974

Gregory Scott and Carol Stover are pictured on the front steps of Doane Hall in 1955. Gregory Scott was one of the first boys to be registered under the new "Country Day School" status. The dramatic changes brought forward by the school in the 1950s had helped the enrollment grow from 101 in 1952 to 211 by 1959.

Among the many athletic pursuits of the students was tennis. The sport had been enjoyed at St. Mary's in earlier decades on a grass court, but the school had added at least one paved court by the 1930s. Because of the growth of the sport's popularity among the students, the school had added two more paved courts by the 1950s.

In the early 1950s, the tumbling team evolved to become the St. Mary's Hall cheerleaders. The girls came out for many competitive events between schools, such as basketball and field hockey games. They also competed with other cheer squads and performed at numerous school events.

Shown here is Margaret Jean Fenimore (class of 1957), who is known to many at the school by her married name, Peggy Morris. After graduating and marrying Robert Morris, she came back to the school to serve as president of the Society of Graduates and, after many years of continued service as a member of the board of trustees, is now trustee emerita of the Trustees of Doane Academy.

Chef Henry Purvis served on the kitchen staff of St. Mary's Hall for over 30 years. During the many functions each year, Purvis could be counted on to amaze the students and faculty with his talents and skills. During the annual Christmas dinner, all waited in anticipation for, among his other creations, his flaming plum pudding.

Commencements in the late 1950s were slightly changed from earlier years, as the bishop no longer presented each student with their diploma. Still, the baccalaureate service maintained some of the oldest traditions of the school. After receiving diplomas, students went outside and planted ivy and then each "willed" their cap and gown to a junior. Later, after dinner, they each sent a lighted candle floating down the Delaware River.

In the spring of 1957, St. Mary's Hall held its first annual horse show. Held at the Helis Stock Farm in Jobstown, New Jersey, the event was created to raise money for a scholarship fund. All ribbons, trophies, and a Revere bowl were donated by parents, friends, and faculty of the school. Alongside the horse show, the students set up a fair where attendees could purchase everything from cakes, to carnation corsages, to glassware, pottery, and jewelry. The show was a success and continued for decades, changing focus in the mid-1960s after a generous former student bequeathed a large sum to the scholarship fund. After that time, the horse show acted as a fundraiser for the improvement of the buildings and grounds of the school.

1st Annual

HORSE SHOW and FAIR

Scholarship Fund

MAY 18, 1957
HELIS FARMS

PRICE 25c

ST. MARY'S HALL

By the mid-1950s, Riverside was no longer used for classroom space and shortly thereafter became a target of vandals. After having to deal with numerous break-ins and literally hundreds of broken panes of glass, the building was eventually boarded up. The trustees began to discuss the possibility of demolishing the old structure. Word got out, and numerous organizations lined up to save the historic building. The Burlington Historical Society offered to lease the building but was rejected when they refused to also pay for restoration and repairs. The National Trust for Historic Preservation and the Smithsonian Institution also lobbied to preserve the building, or at least sections of it, such as the unique library and staircase balustrades. For reasons that remain unclear, the offers were rejected and sadly, Riverside was demolished in June 1961.

The chapel organ, which had not seen any extensive maintenance work since the beginning of the century, was internally refurbished in 1962 by the Edgar H. Mangam's pipe organ company. The organ was refelted, and new leather buttons and slide tuners were installed. The unit was also cleaned and tuned. In 2011, the organ finally underwent a full and proper restoration, completed by Patrick J. Murphy and Associates Pipe Organ Builders.

An exciting program was begun in 1962. St. Mary's Hall, which previously had an informal relationship with her sister school, the St. Mary's Hall of Brighton, England, now initiated a formal exchange program. A student from each school was sent across the Atlantic to spend a full year at the other school. This enriching exchange program continued each year into the early 1970s.

Despite its Episcopal origins, St. Mary's Hall welcomed (and welcomes) students and faculty of all faiths. In one catalog from the 1950s, it was noted that at least nine different faiths were represented within the student body. The long-standing tradition of the *Christmas Mystery* continued on, and even though they did not act in the show, the growing Jewish student population often helped behind the scenes.

In 1953, Elsie Flounders arrived from Jenkintown, Pennsylvania, where she had been president of the school board, to become the school's principal, a position she would hold for over 20 years. In her first decade at the hall (besides getting remarried and becoming "Mrs. Slater"), she oversaw transitions from boarding school to day school and church school to independent school and helped to drive enrollment to over 260 by 1963.

Enrollment continued to grow into the mid-1960s, and pressure began to mount from parents who wanted the school to allow their boys to continue through to the high school level and to graduation. The board began to seriously consider expansion. Pictured is Mrs. Penton's crowded first-grade classroom.

And so the discussion began. In an institution with such a long tradition of being a girls' school, what would happen if it suddenly became completely coeducational? What would Bishop Doane think? The answer came in the form of two separate upper schools, one for boys only and one for girls only, not all that different from what Doane had overseen during the days of Burlington College.

With the board's approval of the opening of a coordinate boys' school to be called Doane Academy, many things had to be worked out, including the need for new physical space for the boys' classes. While it was decided to temporarily house the boys' classes in the second floor of Odenheimer and Doane Halls, construction was begun at the southern end of the campus on new buildings that would introduce new gymnasium space for both schools and would eventually provide the classrooms for the boys' school. The new field house was completed in time to welcome the first students of Doane Academy in the fall of 1966.

Shown here is the dedication ceremony with New Jersey senator Edwin Forsythe placing the cornerstone, inside of which students and faculty had placed mementos of the school's history.

William H. Williams became the first headmaster of the newly opened Doane Academy, although Elsie Slater still oversaw the general operations of both schools. The new school started with grades six through nine and added a new grade each year until the full upper school was complete. Although they shared some of the same spaces, such as the chapel, the music room, and the new gymnasium, schedules were arranged so that the schools were kept separated. In the student *Ivy Leaves* of November 1966, one of the St. Mary's girls lamented that the school year began with a new "don't." In capital letters, the new regulation warned, "DO NOT FRATERNIZE WITH THE DOANE BOYS."

Doane Academy quickly established a rich athletic program, at least in part to help with the recruiting of new students. The field house gym included a full-sized basketball court, and the space was designed so that it could be walled-off into two rooms, if necessary. The new building also contained a fully equipped weight and exercise room, showers, and a locker room. Outside, the board had decided to demolish the Fairholm building and to create a new, full-sized soccer pitch on the property. Among the sporting activities Doane Academy offered were baseball, basketball, soccer, crew, wrestling, and even separate middle and upper school ski clubs.

Doane Academy took off immediately, and its success helped the two schools to reach a combined enrollment of 352 by 1969, the largest student body to date. With this growth came the next phase, the enlargement of the physical plant. In early 1969, ground was broken on a new science building to be attached to the west end of the new gymnasium. Designed during the height of the space race and a national educational focus on science and engineering, the building was designed to hold four laboratories with lecture facilities. It would also have classrooms for chemistry, physics, and biology. Here, Principal Slater is checking on the progress of construction.

On September 21, 1969, the new science building was dedicated. The guest speaker was the Honorable William T. Cahill, elected governor of New Jersey just six weeks later. It was noted in the *Ivy Leaves* that after his speech, Cahill left Burlington to resume campaigning via a helicopter, which had been parked on the soccer field. The science building remains largely unchanged in its uses to this day. There has been a recent additional surge in interest in the sciences at the school, as an engineering and robotics club has recently been added and Summer Academy courses in engineering have been made available to the students.

The initial design to keep the students of St. Mary's Hall and Doane Academy apart proved to be a difficult one. Signs that the walls dividing the two separate schools were coming down can be seen here, as the Drama Club of St. Mary's Hall welcomed boys to join in on their production of *Pygmalion*.

The first graduating class of Doane Academy received their diplomas in a ceremony held on June 9, 1969. President of the board of trustees of Burlington College William J. Youngs presented diplomas to, from left to right, John Abbott, Fred Dolittle, Frank Sleeper, and Thomas Rose, who then also received their ribbons and medals from the Society of Graduates.

As the two schools moved into the 1970s, there was an obvious struggle between the past traditions and the current landscape of the school and the nation as a whole. Although many of the alumni resisted it, more change was coming. Pictured is Betty Fell Seigrist (class of 1923) showing her class ring and sharing memories with some girls of the class of 1971.

Starting in 1971, the board began to discuss the advantages of merging the two schools into one coeducational institution. Among the advantages would be increased class choices for both the boys and girls. After receiving mostly positive responses from a questionnaire that had been sent to parents, it was decided to begin merging the schools. By 1974, the combined schools were known as St. Mary's Hall/Doane Academy.

The Doane Academy class of 1972, pictured here, wanted to leave a gift to the school. They found opportunity in some rusty gates. These gates were originally part of a grand side entrance to the school, known as Scarborough Gate, which had been erected in 1915. In 1952 at the request of the Burlington City fire marshal, the gates were dismantled because newer ladder trucks could not clear the low height of the gates' opening. The gates were left aside, rusting and forgotten, for 20 years. The class of 1972 began the reconstruction of the gate, now on the edge of the soccer field, but it was not completed until the following fall, with the help of the Doane class of 1973.

The gates are now used in the baccalaureate ceremony each year, opening for graduating seniors to pass through.

Like 1837 and 1952, the year 1974 is one that marks a great delineation of eras at the school. Besides the fact that this was the year that saw the school officially change to St. Mary's Hall/Doane Academy, a fully integrated coeducational school, the year was also marked with a devastating fire that affected the course of the school for a generation or more.

Seven

1974–1999

On Wednesday, February 27, 1974, the facade of (and everything else about) the school changed dramatically. At about 8:00 that morning, a fire broke out in the area of the student lounge, on the third floor of Doane Annex. The fire quickly spread across the roof, and soon old Doane Hall's third floor and roof were also in flames. At about 9:00 a.m., the roof of Doane Annex completely collapsed.

A total of nine area fire companies took part in battling the blaze and securing the scene. The Bristol Fire Department was severely delayed in arriving by a bridge opening. The fire was finally extinguished about 10:00 a.m. A firefighter received minor injuries after being hit on the arm and face by melted tar. Doane Annex was all but destroyed by the fire, and Doane Hall sustained severe damage while Scarborough Hall received moderate water damage. Thankfully, the historic chapel and Odenheimer Hall were left undamaged. While a final determination was never made, investigators strongly suspected arson as the cause of the blaze.

The school community rallied and began cleanup and reorganization immediately. Besides the numerous priceless antiques and a pre-Cubism Picasso, six classrooms, the infirmary, a kindergarten classroom, the library, administrative offices, a workshop, and the lounge were lost in the fire. Faculty, parents, friends, and students salvaged and cleaned as much as they could and polished the water-stained floor of the dining hall. New class and library spaces were set up, some in unorthodox areas, such as in the old gym on the third floor of Scarborough Hall, and the school was ready to reopen within a week. Sadly, the remains of Doane Annex had to be demolished, and Doane Hall was boarded up, pending insurance claims and restoration plans.

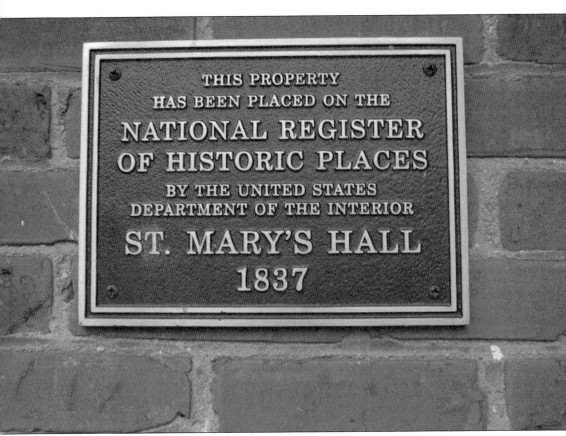

In 1974, as the nation's bicentennial approached, there was a sudden surge in interest in preserving the historic sites of the nation. The National Park Service surveyed the older structures of Burlington and then designated a new Historic District within the city. As a result of this survey, St. Mary's Hall/Doane Academy was added to the National Register of Historic Places in March 1975. The school was selected to join the historic district, at least in part, because of its architectural significance, its importance in the history of women's education, and how it related to church schools in American history.

As the school recovered from the devastating fire of 1974, the entire layout and use of spaces throughout the school were closely examined. The combination study hall/auditorium that was located on the first floor of Odenheimer Hall was temporarily repurposed into an administrative hall, as seen here. Within three years, the space was completely remodeled and reconstructed, creating several new classrooms, offices, and a reception area.

In the place of Doane Annex, which had been attached to Scarborough Hall, rose a new two-story structure housing a multipurpose room on the ground floor, and a classroom and office on the second floor. Also, a portion of the basement of Scarborough Hall was excavated and opened up for use as two lower school classrooms. This space is now used, in part, as the upper school's student union.

In this time of reexamining the best use of spaces at the school, when engineers and architects were estimating the costs of repairs and replacements, the idea of a new master plan arose. According to the 1976 plan, Doane Hall and Odenheimer Hall would have been demolished, and several new buildings would have risen in their place, including a new lower school, auditorium, campus center, Jeffersonian arcade, and swimming pool. The implementation of the plan, which was to take 12 years and millions of dollars to complete, was later canceled because it was decided that the modest sums that were raised would be better spent to meet the immediate needs in the education of the students.

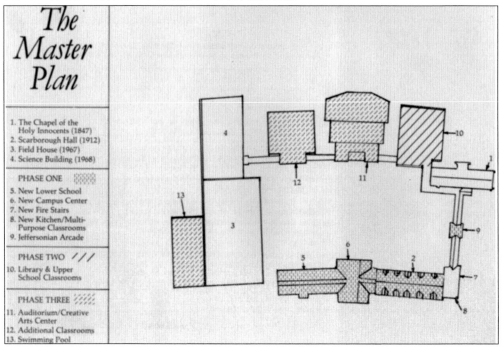

The Master Plan

1. The Chapel of the Holy Innocents (1847)
2. Scarborough Hall (1912)
3. Field House (1967)
4. Science Building (1968)

PHASE ONE
5. New Lower School
6. New Campus Center
7. New Fire Stairs
8. New Kitchen/Multi-Purpose Classrooms
9. Jeffersonian Arcade

PHASE TWO
10. Library & Upper School Classrooms

PHASE THREE
11. Auditorium/Creative Arts Center
12. Additional Classrooms
13. Swimming Pool

Guiding the school through these enormous transitions was the Reverend Dr. William P. Scheel, who had been hired as headmaster shortly after the resignation of Slater in 1974. Dr. Scheel was active in all levels of the school's administration, developing curriculum and college placement programs, guiding the Parent Faculty Association in their new venture of opening a thrift shop on Broad Street, organizing the new master plan, and also creating and teaching a new course for seniors called Family Life. This course was meant to prepare the students for the practical elements of adult life. In this course, students were instructed in values clarification, budgets, banking, leases, and other issues that they might face in college and afterwards.

Through the trials and the aftermath of the fire, the annual horse show and fair continued to grow. By the 1970s, it had found a new home at Maple Beach, the open land on the Pennsylvania side of the Delaware River opposite the school. Local celebrities, such as television reporter Don Tollefson (then of ABC 6 Action News), were among the hosts and ringmasters of the activities. Besides the horse competitions, there were also other attractions, such as three-legged races, obstacle courses, car shows, petting zoos, craft exhibits, and raffle tickets being sold with one year's grand prize being an actual foal. Pictured below enjoying a water ice between events is student Robin Winzinger. Interest in the horse show waned in the 1980s, and the last show took place in 1984.

Rev. Peder Bloom, who began work at St. Mary's Hall/Doane Academy as a history teacher in 1975, was an interesting character and apparently very superstitious. The story told is that a school sports team won a game in which they were great underdogs, and Bloom noted that he was wearing red socks to the game that day, so they must have been lucky socks. From that day forward, he wore only red socks. In 1980, shortly after Dr. Scheel had resigned to take another job, Reverend Bloom was called to a meeting of the board of trustees. When he arrived and noticed that all of the board members were wearing red socks, he realized that he had been chosen as the new headmaster. Reverend Bloom held the post until his sudden passing in April 1984.

Dr. John "Doc" LaVia came to the school from Rutgers University in 1977, hired to teach English. In the next 13 years, he also took up the mantle of college guidance counselor, dean of students, and baseball coach. While he is remembered as a friend and mentor to those who knew him, he may also be considered a model for the current faculty who pride themselves on "wearing many hats."

In 1980, Kathy Lisehora joined the staff as the school nurse, although she and her husband, Wayne, had already been part of the family since their daughter Kathleen entered the school in 1975. Kathy Lisehora has continued as the school nurse, health teacher, and overall loving mother figure to everyone at the school for over 30 years. Her daughter is now development director, and her two grandsons are students at the school.

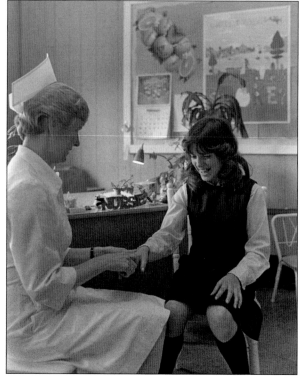

Begun in the dark days of World War II, the tradition of hosting students from England was later continued with an exchange program with St. Mary's Hall of Brighton England. When the decision was made here to integrate into a fully coeducational school, St. Mary's of Brighton (which was still an all-girls' school) decided to end the program. St. Mary's Hall/ Doane Academy then began a new program of their own, exchanging students with other schools in England and France. In 1980, the school began a grand exchange program with the Headlands School of Bridlington (seen here), in the county of York, England, where a dozen or more students at a time crossed the Atlantic. Although the school no longer has a student exchange program with Bridlington, Doane Academy now has a vibrant international student hosting program.

Doane's Dungeon, a Halloween tradition at the school, was begun by the Drama Club in 1984. For three nights each year, students put on a haunted house for the community by acting out scenes from the literary works of William Shakespeare, Edgar Allan Poe, Mary Shelley, and others. As part of the evening's events, guests can sip hot cider and enjoy snacks by the hearth in the dining hall.

Dr. James Paradis joined the faculty in 1987. Through the school's Interim Program (in which regular classes were suspended in favor of upper school students taking multiple-day trips to study, learn, and work, often for charitable causes), "Dr. P" has taken groups of students to Gettysburg and Harper's Ferry not only to learn Civil War history, but also to work hands-on in the preservation and restoration of these historic sites.

The *Christmas Mystery* continues on to this day with one slight change from its original form. An actual infant—a child of the faculty, staff, or one of the school parents—began to be featured in the production starting in 1986. The author's youngest daughter made her own stage debut as the baby Jesus at the tender age of three weeks in 2002. The *Christmas Mystery* is now performed twice: once for the students of the school and a second show given in the evening for parents, alumni, and friends of the school. Pictured here is the 1987 production with Chancellor Van Sciver (class of 1988, walking below), now Doane Academy's chief financial officer.

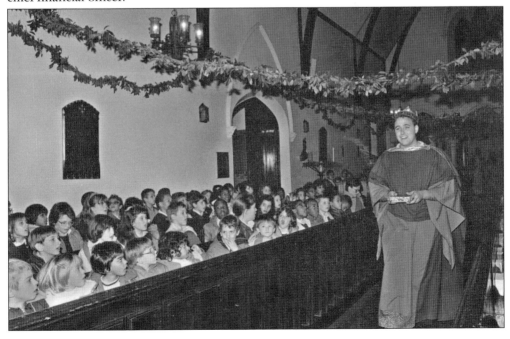

The cheer squad and the rest of the school had more and more to cheer about as the 1980s moved into the 1990s. The school was now fielding teams in baseball, basketball, soccer, cross-country, tennis, softball, and crew.

In 1990–1991, the school began a junior division sports program, which allowed students as young as sixth grade to develop their sporting skills. In the 1991–1992 school year, the boys' and girls' crew teams each reached new heights, as they won multiple championships. The girls' crew won the Philadelphia City Championship and the New Jersey State Championship while the boys' team also won the Philadelphia and New Jersey championships and took first place in the Shipley Regatta.

Pictured on Founder's Day 1993 is Mabel Welles Owen (class of 1933), visiting the school for her 60th reunion. Owen's life and family history are intertwined with the school. Her great-grandfather had been a close friend of Bishop Doane. Her grandmother Harriet Randolph attended and graduated from St. Mary's Hall. Owen and her sister Muriel both graduated from the school, and Bishop Matthews, a close friend of her father's, had paid their tuition expenses. Owen kept up correspondence with the school, and in a 2008 letter (written when she was 93), she reminisced about her fond memories of the school and in particular how "Miss Spurr used to read to us Sunday evenings and sometimes she would read rules or activities from the early days of the school." Owen passed away in June 2010.

In the summer of 1994, the original building of St. Mary's Hall, known as Doane Hall, suffered its final insult in the form of a severe storm, which took down a large portion of the east wall. The building, boarded up since the 1974 blaze, had gone through numerous surveys and estimates of repair. When it was discovered that the building had serious preexisting structural problems that would cost nearly $1 million to repair, the school debated about the finances and how to best deal with the historic structure. After the storm, the building was condemned by the city and sadly had to be demolished. A portion of Nelson Corridor, which ran along the back of Doane Hall, was preserved and remodeled into a beautiful new entrance for the school.

Eight

1999–2012

The complete loss of Doane Hall had opened a breech between the school trustees and administration and many of the alumni and former supporters of the school. Over the course of the remaining years of the 20th century, the school suffered financially and struggled to rediscover its identity and to reset its course and goals. The events of 1999–2000 mark an end and the beginning of a new journey.

Beginning in 1974, the school faced years of tremendous expense to recover from the fire, and after the final loss of Doane Hall in 1994, the school's support and financial backing by many alumni and other friends was severely strained. Some of the alumni were devastated that Doane Hall, the original building of the school, was not rescued, and they severed their relationship with and financial support for the school. As a result of these cumulative problems that began in 1974, the school was nearly lost forever. In fact, in the summer of 1999, the trustees voted to close the school. The school was saved by a public loan arranged by state senator Diane Allen and by the rallying of alumni and community, who realized the true importance of St. Mary's Hall. The school's resurgence had begun.

In June 2000, John F. McGee was recruited as the new headmaster. McGee brought with him great enthusiasm, optimism, and over 30 years of educational experience. He was quick to meet with trustees, faculty, and students to clarify the image and direction of the school. His first challenge to students came in a chapel service where he asked of them, "Who are you? What are your talents? What are you going to do about it?" All involved with the school were asked to apply the best of themselves to their everyday lives and to the school. Among the new traditions begun in McGee's first year were the senior class canoe trip on the Delaware to open the school year and school families (groups of faculty and students from across all grades meeting once per week as peer groups).

Over the next few years, the school reinstated old traditions and began some new ones while further developing their sports and academic programs. During this same time, faculty, parents, and students grew to take real ownership in the direction and growth of all aspects of the school. Martin Luther King Jr. Day was changed from a school holiday to a day of service where the school's students work with charities, such as Habitat for Humanity and Special Olympics, on projects, including cleaning up parks and historic sites. In another of the newer traditions, dozens of students and parents ride in the annual 100-mile Ride Onward Scholarship Bike Challenge.

Developing character and leadership skills has become a deep focus of the school from the prekindergarten program all the way through to graduation.

On September 11, 2001, classes were interrupted by news of the terrorist attacks on New York, the Pentagon, and in Pennsylvania. An all-school convocation in the chapel was immediately called together by John McGee. Students were told of how the nation had suffered great calamities before, like the attack at Pearl Harbor, and how the nation had overcome such trying times. The convocation closed with the singing of "God Bless America" and the "Star-Spangled Banner." The following day, the varsity boys' soccer team traveled to Morristown. When referees refused to let Kulwinder Gill (class of 2002, pictured at right) play because of his Sikh turban, his teammates showed their character and understanding of events by refusing to play without him. Seeing the resolve of the "Men of St. Mary's," as McGee came to call them, the other team refused to play as well.

After the demolition of Doane Hall, the former side entrance to the school, on the western side of Odenheimer Hall, grew to become the de facto main entrance to the school. This old side entrance was poorly modified at some point many years earlier to serve as an entrance, fire escape, and storage shed. As the school was now making new strong statements, it was noticed by Alice Collins Fisk (class of 1961) that this entrance was making a weak statement. Fisk, and her husband, Bernard, initiated and contributed to a fundraising effort that with the contributions and volunteer work of many others, resulted in the 2003 ribbon-cutting ceremony at the portico that now bears their name. The old chapel bell, hung in the Fisk Portico, peals to open each school day and is also rung at commencement.

The name *Saint Mary's Hall/Doane Academy* and even the abbreviated *SMH/DA* had always been a mouthful and in 2008 was looked to as a contributor to the public's confusion over just what the school actually was. For those outside of the school, questions had abounded for decades. Was St. Mary's a Roman Catholic school? Was it a seminary? Was it an orphanage? In this new era of bold action and after consulting many alumni, it was decided by the board to rename the school to honor its past and to reach eagerly toward the future. The name *Doane Academy* was selected at least in part to illustrate the school's resolve to honor its founder and to continue his visionary, leading-edge approach to education. It was also hoped that this new name would help to clear the previous misconceptions of the school.

In 2005, the school received a historic preservation grant that led to detailed studies and assessments of the structures of the school. The final report, released in October 2007 by Westfield Architects and Preservation Consultants, advocated for the demolition of Nelson Corridor, the Chapel Annex, and another connector building often referred to as the infirmary. These buildings, used as little more than connector hallways for many years, were deemed of insignificant historic value. They were also determined to be structurally unsound as a result of having been altered and re-altered so many times over the decades. In the summer of 2010, thanks to an in-kind gift worth $250,000 given by the Robert Winzinger family, these buildings were razed, exposing the eastern outer wall of the chapel for the first time ever. The chapel wall went through extensive renovation and was completed in late 2011.

At the time of the publishing of this book, plans were in the works to rebuild old Doane Hall, as depicted here. This new structure, designed by architect John Martin, would replicate the external appearance and dimensions of the original building but would be of the latest technology and utility on the inside. The new building would have a new Nelson Corridor behind it and also have two- and three-story additions on either side of this main structure. With the aid of a new elevator, wheelchair access across the majority of the rooms on campus would be available for the first time. It has been suggested that this re-creation of the original structure of St. Mary's Hall may itself be named St. Mary's Hall. (Courtesy John G. Martin, architect.)

The tradition of the senior class arriving by canoe on the first day of school continues to evolve and gain greater weight and meaning each year. In September 2000, the canoe ride consisted of the headmaster and the president of the senior class paddling the mile or so from the Red Dragon Canoe Club. By 2011, this had become the Senior Sojourn, a three-day, rain-or-shine experience of bonding, biking, camping, community service, and of course canoeing along the Delaware, accompanied by bagpiper Curt Anderson on a police boat. Seniors are greeted at the school by parents, students, friends, and others from the community. It is a moving experience for all, as the canoes often emerge out of a foggy mist on the river while strains of "Amazing Grace" echo along the water.

The first decade of the millennium witnessed much for the school community to be proud of. The music program grew greatly under the late Ron Bennett (1937–2011), who founded what would later be described as "a world class concert program" among other accomplishments during his 10 years at Doane. His legacy is carried forward through the efforts of Adrienne Mazar and Dr. Shelley Zuckerman. Musical instruction, once considered an "extra," is now built in to tuition.

Athletic programs have also thrived, as is demonstrated most recently by the 2011 Penn-Jersey title won by the girls' varsity soccer team and the school's recent admission to the New Jersey Interscholastic Athletic Association (NJSIAA), giving Doane Academy sports teams the chance to compete for state championships for the first time. Sparty, the school's mascot, has a lot to be excited about!

Continuing with Bishop Doane's original example, Doane Academy prides itself on exceeding standards and expectations and is moving the bar higher once again. In 2011, the school partnered with Hearts in Motion, a nonprofit organization that previously worked only with people of college age and above, to organize a student service trip to Guatemala. Instructor Alyssa Jerdon and nine of her advanced Spanish-language students spent a week in the poorest sections of Guatemala distributing over 1,000 pounds of donations from the Doane community, pouring foundations for a nutrition center, painting a hospital, serving meals, and doing a number of other volunteer projects. It can be said that the school has taken to heart a quote by Mahatma Gandhi: "Be the change you want to see in the world."

Much of the school's recent transformation—from the expanded science and engineering programs and the opening of a second art studio on the third floor of Odenheimer Hall, to the overall improvements in physical plant and expanded opportunities for students—is thanks in no small part to the generous support and vision of Mr. and Mrs. Henry Rowan, the Rowan Family Foundation, the Susquehanna Foundation, and countless other friends of Doane Academy. Pictured are Mr. and Mrs. John McGee (left) and Mr. and Mrs. Henry Rowan (right).

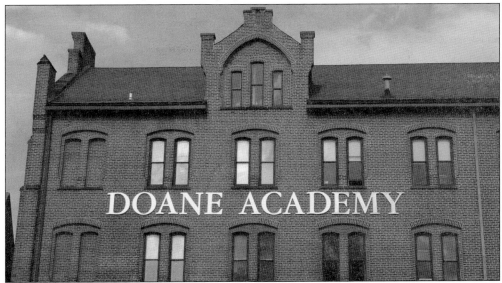

And so, this little school by the Delaware River, opened with great love and high aspirations, which has survived trials of finance, war, disease, and fire, moves Right Onward with a renewed sense of identity and purpose. In 1837, Bishop Doane opened a school that immediately changed the world of education for women, and now Doane Academy continues his visionary efforts as it challenges all to "Change the World!"

DISCOVER THOUSANDS OF LOCAL HISTORY BOOKS FEATURING MILLIONS OF VINTAGE IMAGES

Arcadia Publishing, the leading local history publisher in the United States, is committed to making history accessible and meaningful through publishing books that celebrate and preserve the heritage of America's people and places.

Find more books like this at
www.arcadiapublishing.com

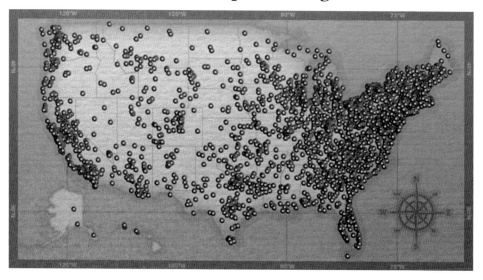

Search for your hometown history, your old stomping grounds, and even your favorite sports team.